George Saville

The Lady's New-year's Gift or Advice to a Daughter

George Saville

The Lady's New-year's Gift or Advice to a Daughter

ISBN/EAN: 9783741180316

Manufactured in Europe, USA, Canada, Australia, Japa

Cover: Foto ©Andreas Hilbeck / pixelio.de

Manufactured and distributed by brebook publishing software (www.brebook.com)

George Saville

The Lady's New-year's Gift or Advice to a Daughter

THE
Lady's New-year's Gift:
OR,
ADVICE
TO A
DAUGHTER.

Under thefe following Heads, *viz.*

RELIGION,
HUSBAND,
HOUSE,
FAMILY and CHILDREN,
BEHAVIOUR and CONVERSATION,
FRIENDSHIP,
CENSURE,
VANITY and AFFECTATION,
PRIDE,
DIVERSIONS.

By the Right Honourable
GEORGE Lord SAVILLE,
Late Marquis and Earl of HALIFAX.

The Fifteenth Edition, exactly Corrected.

LONDON:
Printed for J. DODSLEY, at *Tully's-Head*, in Pall-Mall. MDCCLXV.

THE
LADY's New-Year's Gift:
OR,
ADVICE
TO A
DAUGHTER.

Dear DAUGHTER,

I FIND, that even our most pleasing Thoughts *will* be unquiet; they *will* be in Motion; and the *Mind* can have no rest whilst it is possess'd by a darling Passion. *You* are at present the chief Object of my *Care*, as well as of my *Kindness*, which sometimes throweth me into *Visions* of your being happy in the World, that are better suited to my partial *Wishes*, than to my reasonable *Hopes* for you. At other times, when my *Fears* prevail, I shrink as if I was struck, at the Prospect of *Danger*, to which a young Woman must be exposed. By how much the more *Lively*, so much the more *Liable* you are to be hurt: as the finest Plants are soonest nipped by the *Frost*. Whilst you are playing full of Innocence, the spiteful World will bite, except you are guarded by your *Caution*. Want of *Care* therefore, my dear Child, is never to be excused; since, as to *this* World, it hath the same Effect as want of *Virtue*. Such an early sprouting Wit requireth so much the more to be shelter'd by some *Rules*, like something strew'd on tender Flowers to preserve them from being blasted. You must take it well to be prun'd by so kind a

Hand

RELIGION.

Hand as that of a *Father*. There may be some Bitterness in meer Obedience: The natural Love of *Liberty* may help to make the Commands of a Parent harder to go down: Some inward Resistance there will be, where *Power* and not *Choice* maketh us move. But when a *Father* layeth aside his Authority, and persuadeth only by his Kindness, you will never answer it to Good-Nature, if it hath not weight with you.

A great Part of what is said in the following *Discourse* may be above the present growth of your Understanding; but that becoming every Day Taller, will, in a little time, reach up to it, so as to make it easy to you. I am willing to begin with you before your Mind is quite form'd, that being the Time in which it is most capable of receiving a *Colour* that will last when it is mixt with it. Few things are well learnt, but by early *Precepts:*

Thofe well infus'd, make them *Natural*; and we are never fure of retaining what is valuable, till by a continued *Habit* we have made it a Piece of us.

Whether my Skill can draw the Picture of a fine Woman, may be a Queftion: But it can be none, That I have drawn that of a kind *Father:* If you will take an exact Copy, I will fo far prefume upon my Workmanfhip, as to undertake you fhall not make an ill *Figure*. Give me fo much Credit as to try, and I am fure that neither your Wifhes nor mine fhall be difappointed by it.

※※※※※※※※※※※※※※※

RELIGION.

THE firft thing to be confidered, is *Religion*. It muft be the chief Object of your Thoughts, fince it would be a vain thing to direct

rect your *Behaviour* in the World, and forget that which you are to have towards him who made it. In a strict Sense, it is the only thing necessary: You must take it into your *Mind*, and from thence throw it into your *Heart*, where you are to embrace it so close as never to lose the *Possession* of it. But then it is necessary to distinguish between the *Reality* and the *Pretence*.

Religion does not consist in believing the Legend of the *Nursery*, where Children with their *Milk* are fed with the Tales of Witches, Hobgoblins, Prophecies and Miracles.

We suck in so greedily these early *Mistakes*, that our riper *Understanding* hath much ado to cleanse our *Minds* from this kind of *Trash*: The Stories are so entertaining, that we do not only believe them, but relate them; which makes the Discovery of the *Truth* somewhat grievous, when it makes us lose such a Field of Impertinence, where we might

have

have diverted ourselves, besides the throwing some Shame upon us for having ever received them. This is making the *World* a *Jest*, and imputing to GOD Almighty, That the Province he assigneth to the Devil, is to play at Blind-man's-buff, and shew Tricks with Mankind; and is so far from being *Religion*, that it is not *Sense*, and hath right only to be called that kind of *Devotion*, of which *Ignorance* is the undoubted *Mother*, without competition or dispute. These Mistakes are therefore to be left off with your Hanging-sleeves, and you ought to be as much out of Countenance to be found with them about you, as to be seen playing with Babies, at an *Age* when other things are expected from you.

The next thing to be observ'd to you, is, That *Religion* doth as little consist in loud Answers and devout Convulsions at Church, or Praying in an extraordinary manner. Some Ladies are so extream stirring at *Church*,

Church, that one would swear the *Worm* in their *Conscience* made them so unquiet. Others will have such a divided Face between a *Devout Goggle*, and an *Inviting Glance*, that the unnatural Mixture maketh even the *best Looks* to be at that time ridiculous. These affected *Appearances* are ever suspected, like very strong Perfumes, which are generally thought no very good Symptoms in those that make use of them. Let your Earnestness therefore be reserved for your *Closet*, where you may have GOD Almighty to yourself: In *Public* be still and calm, neither undecently *Careless*, nor *Affected* in the other Extream.

It is not true Devotion, to put on an angry *Zeal* against those who may be of a different Persuasion; *Partiality* to ourselves makes us often mistake it for a *Duty*, to fall hard upon others in that Case; and being push'd on by *Self-conceit*, we strike without Mercy, believing that the *Wounds* we give are *Meritorious*, and that we are fighting GOD ALMIGHTY's Quarrel; when the Truth is, we are only setting out ourselves. Our *Devotion* too often breaketh out into that *Shape* which most agreeth with that particular *Temper*. The *Cholerick* grow into a hardened Severity against all who dissent from them; snatch at all the Texts of Scripture that suit with their *Complexion*; and because GOD's Wrath was some time kindled, they conclude, That *Anger* is a Divine Virtue; and are so far from imagining their ill-natur'd *Zeal* requireth an *Apology*, that they value themselves upon it, and triumph in it. *Others*, whose Nature is more *Credulous* than ordinary, admit no Bounds or Measure to it; they grow as proud of extending their *Faith*, as Princes are of enlarging their *Dominions*; not considering, that our *Faith*, like our *Stomach*, is capable of being overcharg'd; and that

that as the last is destroyed by taking in more than it can digest, so our *Reason* may be extinguished by oppressing it with the Weight of too many strange things; especially if we are forbidden to chew what we are commanded to swallow. The *Melancholy* and the *Sullen*, are apt to place a great part of their *Religion* in dejected or ill-humour'd *Looks*, putting on an unsociable Face, and declaiming against the innocent Entertainment of *Life*, with as much Sharpness as they could bestow upon the greatest Crimes. This generally is only a *Vizard*, there is seldom any thing real in it. No other thing is the better for being *Sour*; and it would be hard that *Religion* should be so, which is the best of things. In the mean time, it may be said with Truth, that this *surly* kind of *Devotion* hath, perhaps, done little less Hurt in the World, by frighting, than the most scandalous *Examples* have done by infecting it.

Having

Having told you in these few Instances, to which many more might be added, what is not true *Religion*; it is time to describe to you what is so. The ordinary *Definitions* of it are no more like it, than the common Sign-posts are like the Princes they would represent. The unskilful *Daubers* in all Ages have generally laid on such ill *Colours*, and drawn such harsh *Lines*, that the Beauty of it is not easily to be discerned: They have put in all the forbidding Features that can be thought of; and, in the first place, have made it an irreconcileable Enemy to *Nature*, when, in reality, they are not only *Friends* but *Twins*, born together at the same time; and it is doing violence to them both, to go about to have them separated. Nothing is so kind and so inviting as true and *unsophisticated Religion*: Instead of imposing unnecessary Burdens upon our *Nature*, it easeth us of the greater weight of our *Passions*, or *Mistakes:* Instead of subduing us with *Rigour*, it redeemeth us from the *Slavery* we are in to ourselves, who are the most severe Masters, whilst we are under the Usurpation of our *Appetites* let loose and not restrained.

Religion is a chearful thing, so far from being always at Cuffs with *Good Humour*, that it is inseparably united to it. Nothing unpleasant belongs to it, though the *Spiritual Cooks* have done their unskilful part to give an ill *Relish* to it. A wise *Epicure* would be *Religious* for the sake of *Pleasure*; good Sense is the Foundation of both; and he is a *Bungler* who aimeth at true *Luxury*, but where they are join'd.

Religion is exalted *Reason*, refined and sifted from the grosser Parts of it. It dwelleth in the upper Region of the *Mind*, where there are fewer *Clouds* or *Mists* to darken or offend it: It is both the Foundation and the Crown of all Virtues: It is

Morality

Morality improved and raised to its Height, by being carried nearer *Heaven*, the only Place where *Perfection* resideth. It cleanseth the *Understanding*, and brusheth off the Earth that hangeth about our *Souls*. It doth not want the *Hopes* and the *Terrors* which are made use of to support it; neither ought it to descend to the borrowing any Argument out of itself, since there we may find every thing that should invite us. If we were to be hired to *Religion*, it is able to out-bid the corrupted World, with all it can offer to us, being so much the *richer* of the two, in every thing where *Reason* is admitted to be a Judge of the Value.

Since this is so, it is worth your Pains to make *Religion* your Choice, and not to make use of it only as a *Refuge*. There are Ladies, who finding by the too visible Decay of their good Looks, that they can shine no more by that *Light*, put on the *Varnish* of an affected Devotion, to keep

keep up some kind of Figure in the World. They take Sanctuary in the *Church*, when they are pursued by growing *Contempt*, which will not be stopt, but followeth them to the *Altar*. Such late Penitence is only a Disguise for the tormenting Grief of being no more handsome. That is the killing Thought which draweth the Sighs and Tears, that appeareth outwardly to be applied to a better End.

There are many who have an *Aguish Devotion*, hot and cold Fits, long Intermissions, and violent Raptures. This Unevenness is by all means to be avoided. Let your Method be a steady Course of good *Life*, that may run like a smooth Stream, and be a perpetual Spring to furnish the continued *Exercise* of *Virtue*. Your *Devotion* may be earnest, but it must be unconstrain'd; and, like other Duties, you must make it your *Pleasure* too, or else it will have very little Efficacy. By
this

this *Rule* you may best judge of your own Heart. Whilst those *Duties* are *Joys*, it is an Evidence of their being sincere; but when they are a *Penance*, it is a sign that your *Nature* maketh some resistance; and whilst that lasteth, you can never be entirely secure of yourself.

If you are often unquiet, and too nearly touched by the cross Accidents of *Life*, your *Devotion* is not of the right *Standard*; there is too much *Allay* in it. That which is right and unmixt, taketh away the *Sting* of every thing that would trouble you: It is like a healing *Balm*, that extinguishes the Sharpness of the Blood: so this softeneth and dissolveth the *Anguish* of the *Mind*. A devout *Mind* hath the Privilege of being free from *Passions*, as some Climates are from all venomous kind of Creatures. It will raise you above the little *Vexations*, to which others, for want of it, will be exposed, and bring you to a *Temper*,

Temper, not of stupid *Indifference*, but of such a wise *Resignation*, that you may live in the *World*, so as it may hang about you like a loose Garment, and not tied too close to you.

Take heed of running into that common *Error*, of applying GOD's Judgments upon particular Occasions. Our Weights and Measures are not competent to make the Distribution either of his *Mercy* or his *Justice*: He hath thrown a Veil over these things, which makes it not only an *Impertinence*, but a kind of *Sacrilege*, for us to give Sentence in them without his *Commission*.

As to your particular *Faith*, keep to the *Religion* that is grown up with you, both as it is best in itself, and that the Reason of staying in it upon that Ground is somewhat stronger for your Sex, than it will, perhaps, be allowed to be for ours, in respect that the voluminous Enquiries into the *Truth*, by Reading, are less expected from you. The
Best

Best of *Books* will be Direction enough to you not to change; and whilst you are fix'd and sufficiently confirm'd in your own *Mind*, you will do best to keep vain *Doubts* and *Scruples* at such a distance, that they may give you no Disquiet.

Let me recommend to you a Method of being rightly inform'd, which can never fail: It is, in short, this: Get *Understanding*, and practise *Virtue*. And if you are so *Blessed* as to have those for your *Share*, it is not surer that there is a GOD, than it is, that by Him all *Necessary Truths* will be reveal'd to you.

HUSBAND.

THAT which challengeth the next place in your Thoughts is, how to live with a *Husband*. And though that is so large a Word, that few *Rules* can be fix'd to it which are

are unchangaeble, the *Methods* being as various as the several *Tempers* of *Men* to which they must be suited; yet I cannot omit some *General Observations*, which, with the Help of your own, may the better direct you in the part of your Life upon which your *Happiness* most dependeth.

It is one of the *Disadvantages* belonging to your *Sex*, that young Women are seldom permitted to make their own *Choice*; their Friends Care and Experience are thought safer Guides to them, than their own *Fancies*: and their *Modesty* often forbiddeth them to refuse when their Parents recommend, though their *inward Consent* may not entirely go along with it. In this Case there remaineth nothing for them to do, but to endeavour to make that easy which falleth to their *Lot*, and by a wise Use of every thing they may dislike in a *Husband*, turn that, by degrees, to be very supportable, which,

which, if neglected, might, in time, beget an *Aversion*.

You must first lay it down for a Foundation in general, That there is *Inequality* in the Sexes, and that for the better Oeconomy of the World, the *Men*, who were to be the Lawgivers, had the larger share of *Reason* bestowed upon them, by which means your Sex is the better prepared for the *Compliance* that is necessary for the better Performance of those *Duties* which seem to be most properly assign'd to it. This looks a little uncourtly at the first Appearance; but, upon Examination, it will be found, that *Nature* is so far from being unjust to you, that she is partial on our Side. She hath made you such large *Amends* by other Advantages, for the seeming *Injustice* of the first Distribution, that the Right of Complaining is come over to our Sex. You have it in your Power not only to free yourselves, but to subdue your Masters,

and

and without Violence throw both their *Natural* and *Legal Authority* at your Feet. We are made of differing *Tempers*, that our *Defects* may the better be mutually supplied: Your *Sex* wanteth our *Reason* for your *Conduct*, and our *Strength* for your *Protection*: Ours wanteth your *Gentleness* to soften and to entertain us. The first Part of our Life is a good deal subjected to you in the *Nursery*, where you reign without Competition, and by that means have the advantage of giving the first *Impressions*. Afterwards you have stronger Influences, which, well managed, have more force on your behalf, than all our *Privileges* and *Jurisdictions* can pretend to have against you. You have more Strength in your *Looks*, than we have in our *Laws*; and more Power by your *Tears*, than we have by our *Arguments*.

It is true, that the *Laws* of *Marriage* run in a harsher Stile towards your

your *Sex*. *Obey* is an ungenteel Word, and less easy to be digested, by making such an unkind Distinction in the Words of the Contract, and so very unsuitable to the Excess of *Good Manners*, which generally goes before it. Besides, the *Universality* of the Rule seemeth to be a *Grievance*, and it appeareth reasonable, that there might be an *Exemption* for extraordinary Women from ordinary Rules, to take away the just Exception that lieth against the false Measure of *general Equality*.

It may be alledged by the *Counsel* retained by your Sex, that as there is in all other Laws an Appeal from the *Letter* to the *Equity*, in Cases that require it; it is as reasonable, that some *Court* of a larger Jurisdiction might be erected, where some *Wives* might resort and plead *specially*. And in such Instances, where Nature is so kind, as to raise them above the *Level* of their own *Sex*, they might have *Relief*, and obtain a *Mitigation* in their own Particular, of a *Sentence* which was given generally againſt *Womankind*. The Cauſes of *Separation* are now ſo very coarſe, that few are *confident* enough to buy their *Liberty* at the Price of having their *Modeſty* ſo expoſed. And for *Diſparity of Minds*, which above all other things requireth a *Remedy*, the *Laws* have made no *Proviſion*; ſo little refined are numbers of Men, by whom they are compil'd. This, and a great deal more might be ſaid to give a Colour to the Complaint.

But the Anſwer to it, in ſhort, is, that the Inſtitution of *Marriage* is too ſacred to admit a *Liberty* of *objecting* to it: That the Suppoſition of yours being the weaker Sex, having without all doubt a good Foundation, maketh it reaſonable to ſubject it to the *Maſculine Dominion*: That no *Rule* can be ſo perfect, as not to admit ſome *Exceptions*: But the Law preſumeth there would be ſo few found

found in this Case, who would have a sufficient Right to such a Privilege, that it is safer some *Injustice* should be *conniv'd* at in a very few Instances, than to break into an Establishment, upon which the Order of human Society doth so much depend.

You are therefore to make your best of what is *settled* by *Law* and *Custom*, and not vainly imagine, that it will be *changed* for your sake. But that you may not be discouraged, as if you lay under the Weight of an *incurable Grievance*, you are to know, that by a *wise* and *dexterous* Conduct, it will be in your Power to relieve yourself from any thing that looketh like a Disadvantage to it. For your better Direction, I will give a hint of the most ordinary *Causes* of *Dissatisfaction* between Man and Wife, that you may be able by such a *Warning* to live so upon your *Guard*, that when you shall be married, you may know how to *cure* your

your *Husband*'s *Mistakes*, and to *prevent* your own.

First then you are to consider, you live in a Time that hath rendered some kind of Frailties so habitual, that they lay claim to large *Grains* of *Allowance*. The World in this is somewhat unequal, and our Sex seemeth to play the *Tyrant* in distinguishing *partially* for ourselves, by making that in the utmost degree *Criminal* in the *Woman*, which in a *Man* passeth under a much *gentler Censure*. The Root and the Excuse of this Injustice, is the Preservation of Families from any *Mixture* which may bring a Blemish to them: And whilst the *Point* of *Honour* continues to be so placed, it seems unavoidable to give your *Sex* the greater share of the Penalty. But if in this it lieth under any *Disadvantage*, you are more than recompens'd, by having the *Honour* of *Families* in your keeping. The Consideration so great a Trust must give you, maketh full

Amends;

Amends; and this Power the World hath lodged in you, can hardly fail to restrain the Severity of an *ill* Husband, and to improve the Kindness and Esteem of a *good* one. This being so, remember, That next to the Danger of *committing* the Fault yourself, the greatest is that of *seeing* it in your *Husband*. Do not seem to look or hear that way: If he is a Man of Sense he will reclaim himself; the Folly of it, is of itself sufficient to cure him: If he is not so, he will be provoked, but not reformed. To expostulate in these Cases, looketh like declaring War, and preparing Reprisals; which, to a *thinking Husband*, would be a dangerous Reflection. Besides, it is so coarse a Reason which will be assigned for a Lady's too great Warmth upon such an Occasion, that Modesty, no less than Prudence, ought to restrain her: Since such an indecent Complaint makes a Wife much more ridiculous, than the Injury that provoked

voked her to it. But it is yet worse, and more unskilful, to *blaze it* in the World, expecting it should rise up in Arms to take her part: Whereas she will find, it can have no other Effect, than that she will be served up in all Companies, as the *reigning Jest* at that time; and will continue to be the common Entertainment, till she is rescued by some *newer Folly* that cometh upon the Stage, and driveth her away from it. The Impertinence of such Methods is so plain, that it doth not deserve the Pains of being laid open. Be assured, that in these Cases your *Discretion* and *Silence* will be the most *prevailing Reproof*. An *affected Ignorance*, which is seldom a *Virtue*, is a great one here: And when your *Husband* seeth how unwilling you are to be uneasy, there is no stronger Argument to persuade him not to be unjust to you. Besides, it will naturally make him more *yielding* in other things: And whether it be to cover or redeem his *Offence*, you may have the good Effects of it whilst it lasteth, and all that while have the most reasonable Ground that can be, of presuming such a Behaviour will at last entirely convert him. There is nothing so glorious to a *Wife*, as a Victory so gain'd: A Man so reclaim'd, is for ever after subjected to her *Virtue*; and her bearing for a time, is more than rewarded by a Triumph that will continue as long as her Life.

The next thing I will suppose is, That your *Husband* may love *Wine* more than is convenient. It will be granted, That though there are Vices of a deeper Dye, there are none that have a greater Deformity than this, when it is not restrained: But with all this, the same Custom which is the more to be lamented for its being so general, should make it less uneasy to every one in particular, who is to suffer by the Effects of it:
So

So that in the first place it will be no new thing if you should have a *Drunkard* for your *Husband*; and there is by too frequent Example Evidence enough that such a thing may happen, and yet a *Wife* may live too without being miserable. *Self-love* dictateth aggravating Words to every thing we feel; *Ruin* and *Misery* are the Terms we apply to whatsoever we do not like, forgetting the Mixture allotted to us by the Condition of human Life, by which it is not intended we should be quite exempt from Trouble. It is fair, if we can escape such a Degree of it as would oppress us, and enjoy so much of the pleasant Part as may lessen the ill Taste of such Things as are unwelcome to us. Every thing hath two Sides; and for our own Ease we ought to direct our Thoughts to that which may be least liable to Exception. To fall upon the *worst Side* of a *Drunkard*, giveth so unpleasant a Prospect, that it is not possible to dwell upon it. Let us pass then to the more *favourable Part*, as far as a *Wife* is concern'd in it.

I am tempted to say (if the Irregularity of the Expression could in Strictness be justified) That a *Wife* is to thank GOD her *Husband* has *Faults*. Mark the seeming Paradox, my Dear, for your own Instruction, it being intended no farther. A *Husband* without *Faults* is a dangerous Observer; he hath an Eye so piercing, and seeth every thing so plain, that it is exposed to his full Censure. And though I will not doubt but that your *Virtue* will disappoint the sharpest Enquiries; yet few Women can bear the having all they say or do, *represented* in the clear Glass of an Understanding without *Faults*. Nothing softeneth the *Arrogance* of our *Nature*, like a Mixture of some *Frailties*. It is by them we are best told, that we must not strike too hard upon others, because

cause we ourselves do so often deserve Blows: They pull our Rage by the Sleeve, and whisper Gentleness to us in our Censures, even when they are rightly applied. The *Faults* and *Passions* of *Husbands* bring them down to you, and make them content to live upon less unequal Terms, than faultless Men would be willing to stoop to; so haughty is Mankind till humbled by common Weakness and Defects, which in our corrupted State contribute more towards the reconciling us to one another, than all the *Precepts* of the *Philosophers* and *Divines*. So that where the *Errors* of our *Nature* make amends for the *Disadvantages* of yours, it is more your part to make use of the *Benefit*, than to quarrel at the *Fault*.

Thus in case a *Drunken Husband* should fall to your Share, if you will be wise and patient, his *Wine* shall be of your Side; it will throw a *Veil* over your Mistakes, and will set out and improve every thing you do, that he is pleased with. Others will like him less, and by that means he may, perhaps, like you the more. When after having dined too well, he is received at home without a *Storm*, or so much as a *reproachful Look*, the *Wine* will naturally work out all in Kindness, which a *Wife* must encourage, let it be wrapped up in never so much Impertinence. On the other Side, it would boil up into *Rage*, if the mistaken *Wife* should treat him roughly, like a certain Thing called a *kind Shrew*, than which the World, with all its Plenty, cannot shew a more senseless, ill-bred, forbidding Creature. Consider, that where the Man will give such frequent Intermissions of the use of his *Reason*, the *Wife* insensibly getteth a Right of *Governing* in the Vacancy, and that raiseth her *Character* and *Credit* in the Family, to a higher Pitch than perhaps could be done under a *sober Husband*,

Husband, who never putteth himself into an Incapacity of holding the *Reins*. If these are not entire *Consolations*, at least they are *Remedies* to some *Degree*. They cannot make *Drunkenness* a *Virtue*, nor a *Husband* given to it a *Felicity*; but you will do yourself no ill Office in the endeavouring, by these Means, to make the best of such a *Lot*, in case it should happen to be yours; and, by the help of a wise Observation, to make that very supportable which would otherwise be a *Load* that would oppress you.

The next Case I will put is, that your *Husband* may be *Cholerick* or *Illhumour'd*. To this may be said, That *passionate* Men generally make amends at the Foot of the Account. Such a Man, if he is angry one Day without any Cause, will the next Day be as kind without any *Reason*. So that by marking how the *Wheels* of such a Man's Head are used to move, you may easily bring over all his Passion to your Party. Instead of being struck down by his Thunder, you shall direct it where and upon whom you shall think it best applied. Thus are the strongest *Poisons* turn'd to the *best Remedies*; but then there must be *Art* in it, and a *skilful Hand*, else the least *bungling* makes it mortal. There is a great deal of nice Care requisite to deal with a Man of this Complexion. *Choler* proceedeth from *Pride*, and maketh a Man so partial to himself, that he swelleth against Contradiction; and thinketh he is lessened if he is opposed. You must in this Case take heed of *increasing the Storm*, by an *unwary Word*, or *kindling the Fire* whilst the Wind is in a Corner which may blow it in your Face: You are dexterously to yield every thing till he beginneth to cool, and then by slow degrees you may rise and gain upon him: Your *Gentleness* well timed, will, like a Charm, dispel his Anger ill placed;

a

a *kind Smile* will *reclaim*, when a *shrill pettish Answer* would *provoke* him; rather than fail, upon such Occasions, when other *Remedies* are too weak, a little *Flattery* may be admitted, which, by being necessary, will cease to be criminal.

If *Ill Humours* and *Sullenness*, and not open and sudden Heat is his Disease, there is a way of treating that too, so as to make it a Grievance to be endured. In order to it, you are first to know, that naturally *good Sense* hath a mixture of *surly* in it: And there being so much *Folly* in the World, and for the most part so triumphant, it giveth frequent Temptations to raise the *Spleen* of Men who think right. Therefore that which may be generally called *ill Humour*, is not always a *Fault*; it becometh one, when either it is wrong applied, or that it is continued too long, when it is not so: For this Reason you must not too hastily fix an ill Name upon that which may
perhaps

perhaps not deserve it; and though the Case should be that your *Husband* might too sourly resent any thing he disliketh, it may so happen that more Blame shall belong to your *Mistake* than to his *Ill Humour*. If a *Husband* behaveth himself sometimes with an *Indifference* that a *Wife* may think offensive, she is in the wrong to put the worst Sense upon it, if by any means it will admit a better. Some *Wives* will call it *Ill Humour* if their *Husbands* change their Style from that which they used whilst they made their first Addresses to them: Others will allow no *Intermission* or *Abatement* in the Expressions of Kindness to them, not enough distinguishing Times, and forgetting that it is impossible for Men to keep themselves up all their Lives to the Height of some *extravagant Moments*. A Man may at some Times be less careful in little Things, without any cold or disobliging Reason for it: As a *Wife* may
be

be too expecting in smaller Matters, without drawing upon herself the Inference of being *unkind.* And if your *Husband* should be really sullen, and have such frequent Fits, as might take away the *Excuse* of it, it concerneth you to have an Eye prepared to discern the first Appearances of cloudy Weather, and to watch when the Fit goeth off, which seldom lasteth long if it is let alone. But whilst the Mind is sore, every thing galleth it; and that maketh it necessary to let the *Black Humour* begin to spend itself, before you come in and venture to undertake it.

If in the Lottery of the World you should draw a *Covetous Husband*, I confess it will not make you proud of your good *Luck*; yet even such a one may be endured too, though there are few Passions more untractable than that of *Avarice*. You must first take care that your *Definitions* of *Avarice* may not be a Mistake.

You are to examine every Circumstance of your *Husband*'s Fortune, and weigh the Reason of every thing you expect from him, before you have Right to pronounce the Sentence. The Complaint is now so general against all *Husbands*, that it giveth great Suspicion of its being often ill-grounded; it is impossible they should all deserve that Censure, and therefore it is certain that it is many times misapplied. He that *spareth* in every thing is an *inexcusable Niggard*; He that *spareth* in nothing, is an *inexcusable Madman*. The *Mean* is, to spare in what is least necessary, to lay out more liberally in what is most required in our several Circumstances. Yet this will not always satisfy. There are *Wives* who are impatient of the Rules of Oeconomy, and are apt to call their *Husband*'s Kindness into question, if any other Measure is put to their Expence than that of their own Fancy. Be sure to avoid this dangerous

ous Error, such a Partiality to yourself, which is so offensive to an understanding Man, that he will very ill bear a *Wife's* giving herself such an injurious *Preference* to all the *Family*, and whatever belongeth to it.

But to admit the worst, and that your *Husband* is really a *Close-handed Wretch*, you must in this, as in other Cases, endeavour to make it less afflicting to you; and first you must observe *seasonable Hours* of speaking, when you offer any thing in opposition to this reigning Humour; a *third Hand* and a *wise Friend* may often prevail more than you will be allowed to do in your own Cause. Sometimes you are dexterously to go along with him in things where you see that the niggardly part of his Mind is most predominant, by which you will have the better Opportunity of persuading him in things where he may be more indifferent. Our *Passions* are very unequal, and are apt to be raised or lessened,

lessened, according as they work upon different Objects; they are not to be stopped or restrained in those things where our Mind is more particularly engaged. In other Matters they are more tractable, and will sometimes give Reason a Hearing, and admit a fair Dispute. More than that, there are few Men, even in this Instance of *Avarice*, so entirely abandon'd to it, that at some Hours, and upon some Occasions, will not forget their Natures, and for that time turn Prodigal. The same Man who will *grudge* himself what is necessary, let his *Pride* be raised and he shall be *profuse*; at another time his *Anger* shall have the same Effect; a Fit of *Vanity*, *Ambition*, and sometimes of *Kindness*, shall open and enlarge his *narrow Mind*; a Dose of Wine will work upon this tough Humour, and for the time dissolve it. Your Business must be, if this Case happeneth, to watch these *critical Moments*, and not let one

one of them slip without making your Advantage of it; And a *Wife* may be said to want *Skill*, if by these Means she is not able to secure herself, in a good measure, against the Inconveniencies this scurvy Quality in her *Husband* might bring upon her, except he should be such an incurable *Monster* as I hope will never fall to your Share,

The last Supposition I will make, is, That if your *Husband* should be *weak* and *incompetent* to make use of the Privileges that belong to him. It will be yielded, that such a one leaveth room for a great many Objections: But GOD Almighty seldom sendeth a *Grievance* without a *Remedy*, or at least such a *Mitigation* as taketh away a great Part of the Sting and the Smart of it. To make such a *Misfortune* less heavy, you are first to bring to your Observation, That a *Wife* very often maketh a better Figure for her *Husband*'s making no great one: And
there

there seemeth to be little Reason, why the same *Lady* that chuseth a *Waiting Woman* with *worse Looks*, may not be content with a *Husband* with *less Wit*; the Argument being equal from the Advantage of the Comparison. If you will be more ashamed in some Cases, of such a *Husband*, you will be less afraid than you would, perhaps, be of a wise one. His *unseasonable Weakness* may, no doubt, sometimes grieve you; but then set against this, that it giveth you the *Dominion*, if you will make the right use of it. It is next to his being dead, in which Case the *Wife* has Right to Administer; therefore be sure, if you have such an Idiot, that none except yourself may have the Benefit of the Forfeiture: Such a Fool is a dangerous Beast, if others have the keeping of him; and you must be very undexterous, if when your *Husband* shall resolve to be an *Ass*, you do not take care he may be your *Ass*. But you must

must go skilfully about it, and above all things, take heed of distinguishing in Public what kind of *Husband* he is: Your inward Thoughts must not hinder the outward Payment of the Consideration that is due to him: Your *slighting* him in *Company*, besides that it would, to a discerning By-stander, give too great Encouragement for the making nearer Applications to you, is in itself such an undecent way of assuming, that it may provoke the tame Creature to break loose, and to shew his *Dominion* for his Credit, which he was content to forget for Ease. In short, the surest and most approved Method will be, to do like a wise *Minister* to an easy *Prince*; first give him the Orders you afterwards receive from him.

With all this, that which you are to pray for, is a *wise Husband*; one that by knowing how to be a *Master*, for that very Reason, will not let

let you feel the Weight of it; one whose Authority is so softened by his Kindness, that it giveth you Ease without abridging your *Liberty*; one that will return so much Tenderness for your *just Esteem* of him, that you will never want *Power*, though you will seldom care to use it. Such a *Husband* is as much above all the other kinds of them, as a rational *Subjection* to a *Prince*, great in himself, is to be preferr'd before the Disquiet and Uneasiness of *Unlimited Liberty*.

Before I leave this Head, I must add a little concerning your *Behaviour* to your *Husband*'s *Friends*, which requireth the most refined Part of your Understanding to acquit yourself well of it. You are to study how to live with them, with more Care than you are to apply to any other Part of your Life; especially at first, that you may not stumble at the first setting out. The *Family* into which you are grafted will generally

nerally be apt to expect, that like a Stranger in a foreign Country, you should conform to their Methods, and not bring in a new Model by your own Authority. The *Friends* in such a Case are tempted to rise up in Arms as against an unlawful Invasion; so that you are with the utmost Caution to avoid the least Appearances of any thing of this kind. And that you may with less Difficulty afterwards give your Directions, be sure at first to receive them from your *Husband*'s Friends. Gain them to you by early applying to them, and they will be so satisfied, that as nothing is more thankful than Pride, when it is complied with, they will strive which of them shall most recommend you: and when they have helped you to take Root in your *Husband*'s good Opinion, you will have less Dependance upon theirs; though you must not neglect any reasonable Means of preserving it. You are to consider, that a
Man

Man governed by his *Friends*, is very easily inflamed by them; and that one who is not so, will yet for his own sake expect to have them considered. It is easily improved to a point of Honour in a *Husband*; not to have his *Relations* neglected; and nothing is more dangerous, than to raise an Objection, which is grounded upon *Pride:* It is the most stubborn and lasting Passion we are subject to, and where it is the first Cause of the *War*, it is very hard to make a secure *Peace*. Your *Caution* in this is of the last Importance to you.

And that you may the better succeed in it, carry a strict Eye upon the *Impertinence* of your Servants; take heed that their *ill Humour* may not engage you to take Exceptions, of their too much assuming in small Matters, raise Consequences which may bring you under a great Disadvantage. Remember that in the Case of a *Royal Bride*, those about her are generally

generally fo far fufpected to bring in a Foreign Intereft, that in moft Countries they are infenfibly reduced to a very fmall Number, and thofe of fo low a Figure, that it doth not admit the being *Jealous* of them. In little and in the Proportion, this may be the Cafe of every *New-married Woman*, and therefore it may be more adviseable for you, to gain the *Servants* you find in a Family, than to tie yourfelf too faft to thofe you carry into it.

You are not to overlook thefe fmall Reflections, becaufe they may appear low and inconfiderable; for it may be faid, that as the *greateft Streams* are made up of the *fmall Drops* at the Head of the Springs from whence they are derived; fo the *greater Circumftances* of your Life will be in fome degree directed by thefe feeming *Trifles*; which having the Advantage of being the firft Acts of it, have a greater Effect than fing-
ly

ly in their own Nature they could pretend to.

I will conclude this Article with my Advice, that you would, as much as Nature will give you leave, endeavour to forget the great Indulgence you have found at home. After such a gentle Discipline as you have been under, every thing you dislike will seem the harsher to you. The Tenderness we have had for you, *my Dear*, is of another nature, peculiar to kind Parents, and differing from that which you will meet with first in any Family, into which you shall be transplanted; and yet they may be very kind too, and afford no justifiable Reason to you to complain. You must not be frighted with the first Appearances of a *differing Scene:* for when you are used to it, you may like the House you go to better than that you left; and your *Husband*'s Kindness will have so much Advantage of ours, that we shall yield up all *Competition*, and

and as well as we love you, be very well contented to surrender to such a *Rival*.

House, Family, *and* Children.

YOU must lay before you, *My Dear*, there are degrees of Care to recommend yourself to the World in the several Parts of your Life. In many things, tho' the doing them well may raise your *Credit* and *Esteem*, yet the Omission of them would draw no immediate Reproach upon you: In others, where your Duty is more particularly applied, the *Neglect* of them is amongst those Faults which are not forgiven, and will bring you under a *Censure*, which will be a much heavier Thing than the Trouble you would avoid. Of this Kind is the *Government* of your *House*, *Family*, and *Children*; which since it is the Province allotted to your Sex, and that the *discharging it well*, will, for that Reason, be expected from you; if you either desert it out of *Laziness*, or manage it ill, for *want of Skill*, instead of a *Help*, you will be an *Incumbrance* to the *Family* where you are plac'd.

I must tell you, that no *Respect* is lasting but that which is produced by our being in some degree useful to those that pay it. Where that faileth, the Homage and the Reverence go along with it, and fly to others where something may be expected in exchange for them. And upon this Principle the *Respects* even of the *Children* and the *Servants* will not stay with one that doth not think them worth their Care; and the old *House-keeper* shall make a better Figure in the *Family*, than the *Lady* with all her fine Cloaths, if she wilfully relinquishes her Title to the *Government*. Therefore take heed of carrying your *good-Breeding* to such a height, as to be good for nothing, and to be proud of it. Some think it hath a great Air to be above troubling their Thoughts with such ordinary Things as their *House* and *Family*; others dare not admit *Cares* for fear they should hasten *Wrinkles*; mistaken *Pride* maketh some think they must keep themselves up, and not descend to these Duties, which do not seem enough refin'd for great *Ladies* to be employ'd in: forgetting all this while, that it is more than the greatest *Princes* can do, at once to preserve Respect, and to neglect their Business. No *Age* ever erected *Altars* to *insignificant Gods*: They had all some *Quality* applied to them to draw *Worship* from *Mankind*; this maketh it the more unreasonable for a *Lady* to expect to be considered, and at the same time resolve not to deserve it. *Good Looks* alone will not do; they are not such a lasting *Tenure* as to be relied upon;

C 2 and

and if they should stay longer than they usually do, it will by no means be safe to depend upon them: For when Time hath abated the Violence of the first liking, and that the *Napp* is a little worn off, though still a good degree of Kindness may remain, Men recover their Sight which before might be dazzled, and allow themselves to object as well as to admire.

In such a Case, when a *Husband* seeth an empty airy Thing sail up and down the House to no kind of Purpose, and look as if she came thither only to make a Visit: When he findeth that after her *Emptiness* hath been extreme busy about some very senseless Thing, she eats her Breakfast half an Hour before Dinner, to be at greater liberty to afflict the Company with her Discourse; then calleth for her Coach, that she may trouble her Acquaintance, who are already cloy'd with her: And having some *proper Dialogues*

logues ready to display her *Foolish Eloquence* at the top of the Stairs, she setteth out like a ship out of the Harbour, laden with Trifles, and cometh back with them: At her Return she repeateth to her faithful Waiting-Woman, the *Triumphs* of that Day's Impertinence; then wrapped up in Flattery and clean Linen, goeth to Bed so satisfied, that it throweth her into pleasant Dreams of her own Felicity. Such a one is seldom serious but with her *Taylor*; her *Children* and *Family* may now and then have a random Thought, but she never taketh aim but at something very impertinent. I say, when a *Husband*, whose Province is without Doors, and to whom the Oeconomy of the House would be in some degree indecent, findeth no *Order* nor *Quiet* in his *Family*, meeteth with *Complaints* of all Kinds springing from this Root; the *mistaken Lady*, who thinketh to make *amends* for all this, by having a well-chosen *Petticoat*, will at last be convinced of her *Error*, and with Grief to be forc'd to undergo the Penalties that belong to those who are wilfully *insignificant*. When this scurvy Hour cometh upon her, she first groweth *angry*; then when the time of it is past, would, perhaps, grow *wiser*, not remembering that we can no more have *Wisdom* than *Grace*, whenever we think fit to call for it. There are Times and Periods fixed for both; and when they are too long neglected, the Punishment is, that they are *irrecoverable*, and nothing remaining but an useless *Grief* for the Folly of having thrown them out of our Power. You are to think what a mean Figure a Woman maketh, when she is so degraded by her own Fault; whereas there is nothing in those Duties which are expected from you, that can be a lessening to you, except your want of *Conduct* makes it so. You may love your *Children* without living

living in the *Nurſery*, and you may have a *competent* and *diſcreet Care* of them, without letting it break out upon the Company, or expoſing yourſelf by turning your Diſcourſe that way; which is a kind of *Laying Children* to the *Pariſh*, and it can hardly be done any where, that thoſe who hear it will be ſo forgiving, as not to think they are overcharged with them. A Woman's *Tenderneſs* to her *Children*, is one of the leaſt deceitful Evidences of her Virtue; but yet the way of expreſſing it, muſt be ſubject to the *Rules* of *good Breeding*: And though a *Woman* of *Quality* ought not to be leſs kind to them, than *Mothers* of the *meaneſt Rank* are to theirs, yet ſhe may diſtinguiſh herſelf in the *Manner*, and avoid the coarſe Methods which in Women of a lower Size might be more excuſable. You muſt begin early to make them love you, that they may obey you. This Mixture is no where more neceſſary than

in Children. And I must tell you, that you are not to expect Returns of Kindness from yours, if you ever have any, without Grains of Allowance; and yet it is not so much a *Defect* in their *good Nature*, as a *Shortness* of *Thought* in them. Their first *Insufficiency* maketh them lean so entirely upon their *Parents* for what is *necessary*, that the *Habit* of it maketh them continue the same *Expectation* for what is unreasonable; and as often as they are *denied*, so often they think they are *injur'd:* And whilst their *Reason*'s yet in the Cradle, their *Anger* looketh no farther than the Thing they long for and cannot have; and to be *displeased* for their *own good*, is a *Maxim* they are very slow to understand: So that you may conclude, the first Thoughts of your *Children* will have no small Mixture of Mutiny; which being so natural, you must not be angry, except you would increase it. You must deny them as seldom as you can, and
when

when there is no avoiding it, you must do it *gently*; you must flatter away their ill Humour, and take the next Opportunity of pleasing them in some other Thing, before they either ask or look for it: This will strengthen your *Authority*, by making it soft to them; and confirm their *Obedience*, by making it their Interest. You are to have as strict a Guard upon yourself amongst your *Children*, as if you were amongst your *Enemies*. They are apt to make wrong Inferences, to take Encouragement from half Words, and misapply what you may say or do, so as either to lessen their *Duty*, or to extend their *Liberty* farther than is convenient. Let them be more in awe of your *Kindness* than of your *Power*. And above all, take heed of supporting a *Favourite Child* in its Impertinence, which will give Right to the rest of claiming the same Privilege. If you have a divided Number, leave the *Boys* to the *Father's* more.

more peculiar Care, that you may with the greater Juſtice pretend to a more immediate Juriſdiction over thoſe of your own Sex. You are to live ſo with them, that they may never chuſe to avoid you, except when they have *offended*, and then let them tremble, that they may diſtinguiſh: But their Penance muſt not continue ſo long as to grow too *ſour* upon their *Stomachs*, that it may not *harden* inſtead of *correcting* them: The kind and ſevere Part muſt have their ſeveral *Turns* ſeaſonably applied; but your *Indulgence* is to have the broader Mixture, that *Love*, rather than *Fear*, may be the Root of their *Obedience*.

Your *Servants* are in the next place to be conſidered; and you muſt remember not to fall into the Miſtake of thinking, that becauſe they receive Wages, and are ſo much *inferior* to you, therefore they are *below* your Care to know how to manage them. It would be as good Reaſon

Reason for a *Master-Workman* to despise the *Wheels* of his *Engines*, because they are made of *Wood*. These are the *Wheels* of your *Family*; and let your Directions be never so faultless, yet if these *Engines* stop or move wrong, the whole Order of your *House* is either at a stand, or discomposed. Besides, the *Inequality* which is between you, must not make you forget, that *Nature* maketh no such Distinction, but that Servants may be looked upon as *humble Friends*, and that *Returns* of *Kindness* and *good Usage*, are as much due to such of them as deserve it, as their *Service* is due to us when we require it. *A foolish Haughtiness* in the style of *speaking*, or in the manner of *commanding* them, is in itself very undecent; besides that it begetteth an *Aversion* in them, of which the least ill Effect to be expected is, that they will be *Slow* and *Careless* in all that is injoined them: And you will find it true by your Experience, that you will

will be so much the more *obey'd* as you are less *imperious*. Be not *too hasty* in giving your Orders, nor *too angry* when they are not altogether *observ'd*, much less are you to be *loud* and too much disturbed: An *Evenness* in distinguishing when they do well or ill, is that which will make your *Family* move by a Rule, and without Noise, and will the better set out your Skill in conducting it with Ease and Silence, that it may be like a well-disciplined Army, which knoweth how to anticipate *Orders* that are fit to be given them. You are never to neglect the Duty of the *present Hour*, to do another Thing, which though it may be better in itself, is not to be unseasonably preferred. Allot well-chosen Hours for the Inspection of your *Family*, which may be so distinguished from the rest of your Time, that the necessary *Cares* may come in their proper Place, without any Influence upon your good Humour,

mour, or Interruption to other Things. By these Methods you will put yourself in Possession of being valued by your Servants, and then their *Obedience* will naturally follow.

I must not forget one of the greatest *Articles* belonging to a *Family*, which is the *Expence*. It must not be such as, by failing either in the Time or Measure of it, may rather draw *Censure* than gain *Applause*. If it was well examined, there is more Money given to be laugh'd at, than for any one Thing in the World, though the Purchasers do not think so. A well stated Rule is like the *Line*, when that is once pass'd, we are under another *Pole*; so the first *straying* from a *Rule*, is a Step towards making that which was before a *Virtue* to change its Nature, and to grow either into a *Vice*, or at least an *Impertinence*. The Art of laying out Money wisely, is not attained to without a great deal of Thought; and it is yet more difficult in the Case of a *Wife*, who is accountable to her *Husband* for her Mistakes in it. It is not only his *Money*, his *Credit* too is at Stake, if what lieth under the Wife's Care, is managed, either with undecent *Thrift*, or too loose *Profusion*. You are therefore to keep the *Mean* between these two *Extreams*; and it being hardly possible to hold the Balance exactly even, let it rather incline toward the *liberal* Side, as more suitable to your Quality, and less subject to *Reproach*. Of the two, a little *Money* mispent is sooner *recovered*, than the *Credit* which is lost by having it unhandsomely *saved*; and a wise *Husband* will less forgive a shameful Piece of *Parsimony*, than a little *Extravagance*, if it be not too often repeated. His *Mind* in this must be your chief *Direction*; and his *Temper*, when once known, will, in a great measure, justify your Part in the Management, if he is pleased with it.

In your *Cloaths* avoid too much Gaudy; do not value yourself upon an *embroidered* Gown; and remember, that a *reasonable Word*, or an *obliging Look*, will gain you more Respect than all your *fine Trappings*. This is not said to restrain you from a *decent Compliance* with the World, provided you may take the wiser, and not the foolisher Part of your Sex for your Pattern. Some *Distinctions* are to be allowed, whilst they are well suited to your *Quality* and *Fortune*; and in the Distribution of the Expence, it seemeth to me that a *full Attendance* and *well-chosen Ornaments* for your House, will make you a better Figure, than *too much glittering* in what you wear, which may with more ease be imitated by those that are below you. Yet this must not tempt you to starve every thing but your own Apartment; or, in order to more Abundance there, give just cause to the least Servant you have, to complain of the want of what is necessary.

neceſſary. Above all, fix it in your Thoughts an unchangeable *Maxim*, That nothing is *truly fine*, but what is *fit*; and that juſt ſo much as is proper for your *Circumſtances* of their ſeveral Kinds, is much finer than all you can add to it. When you once break through theſe Bounds, you launch into a wide Sea of *Extravagance*; every thing will become neceſſary, becauſe you have a mind to it; not becauſe it is *fit* for you, but becauſe ſomebody elſe *hath it*. This *Lady*'s *Logick* ſetteth Reaſon upon its Head, by carrying the *Rule* from *Things* to *Perſons*, and appealing from what is *Right*, to every Fool that is in the *Wrong*. The Word *Neceſſary* is miſerably applied; it diſordereth *Families* and overturneth *Government*, by being ſo abuſed. Remember that *Children* and *Fools* want every thing, becauſe they want Wit to diſtinguiſh; and therefore there is no ſtronger Evidence of a *crazy Underſtanding*, than the making too large a Catalogue

logue of Things neceſſary, when, in truth, there are ſo very few Things that have a right to be placed in it. Try every thing firſt in your *Judgment*, before you allow it a place in your *Deſire*; elſe your *Husband* may think it as neceſſary for him to deny, as it is for you to have whatever is unreaſonable; and if you ſhall too often give him that Advantage, the Habit of *Refuſing* may, perhaps, reach to things that are not unfit for you.

There are unthinking *Ladies*, who do not enough conſider, how little their own Figure agreeth with the *fine Things* they are ſo proud of. Others, when they have them, will hardly allow them to be viſible; they cannot be ſeen without *Light*, and this is many times ſo ſaucy and ſo prying, that like a too forward *Gallant*, it is to be forbid the *Chamber*. Some, when you are uſhered into their *Dark Ruelle*, it is with ſuch Solemnity that a Man would ſwear

there

there were something in it, till the *Unskilful Lady* breaketh Silence, and beginneth a Chat, which discovereth it is a Puppet-Play with magnificent Scenes. Many esteem things rather as they are hard to be gotten, than that they are worth getting: This looketh as if they had an Interest to pursue that Maxim, because a great Part of their own *Value* dependeth upon it. Truth in these Cases would be often *unmannerly*, and might derogate from the *Prerogative* great *Ladies* would assume to themselves, of being distinct Creatures from those of their Sex, which are inferior, and of less difficult Access.

In other things too, your Condition must give the Rule to you, and therefore it is not a *Wife*'s Part to aim at more than a bounded *Liberality*; the farther Extent of that *Quality* (otherwise to be commended) belongeth to the *Husband*, who hath better Means for it. *Generosity* wrong placed becometh a *Vice:* It is no more

more a *Virtue* when it groweth into an *Inconvenience*. *Virtues* must be inlarged or restrained, according to differing Circumstances. A *princely Mind* will undo a *private Family*: Therefore things must be suited, or else they will not deserve to be commended, let them in themselves be never so valuable: And the Expectations of the World are best answered, when we acquit ourselves in that manner which seemeth to be prescrib'd to our several Conditions, without usurping upon those Duties, which do not so particularly belong to us.

I will close the Consideration of this *Article* of *Expence*, with this short Word: Do not *fetter* yourself with such a Restraint in it as may make you *remarkable*; but remember that *Virtu* is the greatest *Ornament*, and good *Sense* the best *Equipage*.

BEHA-

Behaviour *and* Conversation.

IT is time now to lead you out of your *House* into the *World*. A dangerous Step! where your Virtue alone will not secure you, except it is attended with a great deal of *Prudence*. You must have both for your Guard, and not stir without them. The Enemy is abroad, and you are sure to be taken, if you are found Straggling. Your *Behaviour* is therefore to incline strongly towards the *reserved Part*; your *Character* is to be immoveably fixed upon that Bottom, not excluding a Mixture of greater Freedom, as far as it may be innocent and well timed. The *Extravagancies* of the Age hath made *Caution* more necessary; and by the same Reason that the too great Licence of ill Men hath by Consequence

quence in many things reſtrained the lawful Liberty of thoſe who did not abuſe it, the unjuſtifiable Freedoms of ſome of your Sex have involved the reſt in the Penalty of being reduced. And though this cannot ſo alter the nature of Things, as to make that *criminal* which is in itſelf *indifferent*; yet if it maketh it *dangerous*, that alone is ſufficient to juſtify the *Reſtraint*. A *cloſe Behaviour* is the fitteſt to receive *Virtue* for its conſtant *Gueſt*, becauſe there, and there only, it can be ſecure. Proper *Reſerves* are the Outworks, and muſt never be deſerted by thoſe who intend to keep the Place; they keep off the Poſſibilities not only of being *taken*, but of being *attempted*; and if a Woman ſeeth Danger, tho' at never ſo remote a Diſtance, ſhe is for that Time to ſhorten her *Line* of *Liberty*. She who will allow herſelf to go to the *utmoſt Extent* of every thing that is *lawful*, is ſo very near going farther,

ther, that those who lie at watch will begin to count upon her.

Mankind, from the double Temptation of *Vanity* and *Desire*, is apt to turn every thing a *Woman* doth to the *hopeful Side*; and there are few who dare to make an impudent Application, till they discern something which they are willing to take for an *Encouragement*. It is safer therefore to prevent such *Forwardness*, than to go about to cure it. It gathereth Strength by the first *Allowances*, and claimeth a Right from having been at any time suffered with Impunity. Therefore nothing is with more Care to be avoided, than such a kind of *Civility* as may be mistaken for *Invitation*; and it will not be enough for you to keep yourself free from any criminal *Engagements*; for if you do that which either raiseth *Hopes* or createth *Discourse*, there is a Spot thrown upon your good Name; and those kind of Stains are the harder to be taken

taken out, being dropped upon you by the *Man*'s *Vanity*, as well as by the *Woman*'s *Malice*.

Most Men are in one Sense *Platonick Lovers*, though they are not willing to own that *Character*. They are so far *Philosophers*, as to allow, that the greatest Part of Pleasure lieth in the *Mind*; and in pursuance of that *Maxim*, there are few who do not place the Felicity more in the Opinion of the World, of their being *prosperous Lovers*, than in the *Blessing* itself, how much soever they appear to value it. This being so, you must be very cautious not to gratify these *Camelions* at the Price of bringing a *Cloud* upon your *Reputation*, which may be deeply wounded, tho' your *Conscience* is unconcern'd.

Your own Sex too will not fail to help the least Appearance that giveth a *Handle* to be ill turned. The best of them will not be displeased to improve their own Value, by laying others under a *Disadvantage*, where there is a fair Occasion given for it. It distinguishes them still the more: Their own *Credit* is more exalted, and like a Picture set off with Shades, shineth more when a *Lady*, either less *Innocent*, or less *Discreet*, is set near, to make them appear so much the brighter. If these lend their Breath to blast such as are so unwary as to give them this Advantage, you may be sure there will be a stronger Gale from those, who, besides *Malice* or *Emulation*, have an *Interest* too, to strike hard upon a virtuous Woman. It seemeth to them that their Load of Infamy is lessened, by throwing part of it upon others: So that they will not only improve when it lieth in their way, but take pains to find out the least Mistake an *innocent Woman* committeth, in Revenge of the Injury she doth in leading a Life which is a Reproach to them. With these you must be extreme *wary*, and neither provoke them

them to be *Angry*, nor invite them to be *Intimate*.

To the *Men* you are to have a *Behaviour* which may secure you, without *offending* them. No ill-bred affected *Shyness*, nor a *Roughness*, unsuitable to your *Sex*, and unnecessary to your *Virtue*; but a Way of Living that may prevent all Course of *Railleries* or *unmannerly Freedoms*; *Looks* that forbid without *Rudeness*, and oblige without *Invitation*, or leaving room for the saucy Inferences Mens Vanity suggesteth to them upon the least Encouragements. This is so very nice, that it must engage you to have a perpetual *Watch* upon your *Eyes*, and to remember that one careless *Glance* giveth more Advantage than a *hundred Words* not enough considered; the *Language* of the *Eyes*, being very much the most significant and the most observed.

Your *Civility*, which is always to be preserved, must not be carried to a *Compliance*, which may betray you

D   into

into irrecoverable Miſtakes. This *French* ambiguous Word *Complaiſance*, hath led your Sex into more Blame, than all other Things put together. It carrieth them by Degrees into a certain Thing, called a *Good kind of Woman*, an *eaſy idle Creature*, that doth neither *Good* nor *Ill* but by *chance*, hath no *Choice*, but leaveth that to the Company ſhe keepeth. *Time*, which by degrees addeth to the Signification of *Words*, hath made her, according to the modern Stile, little better than one who thinketh it a *Rudeneſs* to deny when civilly required, either her *Service in Perſon*, or her *friendly Aſſiſtance* to thoſe who would have a *Meeting*, or want a *Confident*. She is a certain Thing always at hand, an eaſy *Companion*, who hath ever great *Compaſſion* for *diſtreſſed Lovers*: She cenſureth nothing but *Rigour*; and is never without a *Plaiſter* for a *wounded Reputation*, in which chiefly lieth her Skill in *Chirurgery*: She ſeldom hath the Pro-

Propriety of any particular *Gallant*, but liveth upon *Brokage*, and waiteth for the Scraps her Friends are content to leave her.

There is another *Character* not quite so criminal, yet not less ridiculous; which is that of a *good-humour'd Woman*, one who thinketh she must always be in a *Laugh*, or a broad *Smile*, because *Good-Humour* is an obliging Quality; thinketh it less ill Manners to talk *impertinently* than to be silent in Company. When such a prating *Engine* rideth *Admiral*, and carrieth the *Lanthorn* in a *Circle of Fools*, a *chearful Coxcomb* coming in for a *Recruit*, the *chattering* of *Monkeys* is a better Noise than such a *Concert* of *senseless Merriment*. If she is applauded in it, she is so encouraged, that, like a *Ballad-singer*, who if commended breaketh his Lungs, she letteth herself loose, and overfloweth upon the Company. She conceiveth that Mirth is to have no Intermission, and therefore she will carry it about with her, though it be to a *Funeral*; and if a Man should put a familiar Question, she doth not know very well how to be angry, for then she would be no more that pretty thing called a *Good humour'd Woman*. This Necessity of appearing at all Times to be so infinitely pleased, is a grievous Mistake; since in a *handsome Woman* that *Invitation* is unnecessary; and in one who is not so, ridiculous. It is not intended by this, that you should forswear *Laughing*; but remember, that *Fools* being always painted in that Posture, it may fright those who are wise from doing it too frequently, and going too near a Copy which is so little inviting; and much more from doing it *loud*, which is an unnatural Sound, and looketh so much like another Sex, that few Things are more offensive. That *boisterous* kind of *Jollity* is as contrary to *Wit* and *Good Manners*, as it is to *Modesty* and *Virtue*. Besides, it is a coarse kind of Quality, that throweth a Woman into a lower Form, and degradeth her from the Rank of those who are more refined. Some *Ladies* speak loud and make a *Noise* to be the more minded, which looketh as if they beat their *Drums* for *Volunteers*; and if by Misfortune none come in to them, they may, not without Reason, be a good deal out of Countenance.

There is one Thing yet more to be avoided, which is, the *Example* of those who intend nothing farther than the Vanity of *Conquest*, and think themselves secure of not having their Honour tainted by it. Some are apt to believe their *Virtue* is too *obscure* and not enough known, except it is exposed to a *broader Light*, and set out to its best Advantage by some publick Trials. These are dangerous Experiments, and generally fail, being built upon so weak a Foundation, as that of a too great *Confidence* in ourselves. It is

as safe to play with *Fire*, as to dally with *Gallantry*. *Love* is a Passion that hath Friends in the Garrison, and for that Reason must by a Woman be kept at such a distance, that she may not be within the Danger of doing the most usual thing in the World, which is conspiring against herself: Else the humble Gallant, who is only admitted as a Trophy, very often becometh the Conqueror; he putteth on the Style of Victory, and from an *Admirer* groweth into a *Master*, for so he may be called from the Moment he is in Possession. The first Resolutions of stopping at good Opinion and Esteem, grow weaker by degrees against the Charms of *Courtship* skilfully applied. A *Lady* is apt to think a Man speaketh so much Reason whilst he is *commending* her, that she hath much ado to believe him in the wrong when he is making Love to her: And when, besides the natural Inducements your Sex hath to be merciful, she is bribed
bed

bed by well-chosen *Flattery*, the poor Creature is in danger of being caught, like a Bird listening to the Whistle of one that hath a Snare for it. *Conquest* is so tempting a Thing, that it often maketh Women mistake Mens *Submissions*; which with all their fair Appearance, have generally less *Respect* than *Art* in them. You are to remember, that Men who say extreme fine Things, many times say them most for their own Sakes; and that the vain Gallant is often as well pleased with his own *Compliments*, as he could be with the *kindest Answer*. Where there is not that *Ostentation*, you are to suspect there is *Design*: And as strong *Perfumes* are seldom used but where they are necessary to smother an unwelcome *Scent*, so *excessive good Words* leave room to believe they are strew'd to cover something, which is to gain Admittance under a Disguise. You must therefore be upon your Guard, and consider, that of the two, *Re-*

spect is more dangerous than *Anger.* It puts even the best Understandings out of their Place for the Time, till their second Thoughts restore them; it stealeth upon us insensibly, and throweth down our *Defences*, and maketh it too late to resist, after we have given it that Advantage. Whereas Railing goes away in Sound; it hath so much Noise in it, that by giving warning it bespeaketh Caution. *Respect* is a slow and sure *Poison*, and like *Poison* swelleth us within ourselves. Where it prevaileth too much it groweth to be a kind of *Apoplexy* in the Mind, turneth quite round, and after it hath once seized the Understanding, becometh *mortal* to it. For these Reasons the safest way is to treat it like a sly Enemy, and to be perpetually upon the watch against it.

I will add one *Advice* to conclude this Head, which is, that you will let every seven Years make some Alteration in you towards the *Graver* side,

side, and not be like the *Girls* of Fifty, who resolved to be always *Young*, whatever *Time* with his Iron Teeth hath determined to the contrary. Unnatural things carry a *Deformity* in them never to be *disguised*; the *Liveliness* of *Youth* in a riper Age, looketh like a *new Patch* upon an *old Gown*; so that a *Gay Matron*, a chearful old *Fool*, may be reasonably put into the List of the *Tamer* kind of *Monsters*. There is a certain Creature called a *Grave Hobby-Horse*, a kind of She-Numps, that pretendeth to be pulled to a Play, and must needs go to *Bartholomew-Fair*, to look after the young Folks, whom she only seemeth to make her Care, in reality she taketh them for her Excuse. Such an old *Butterfly* is of all *Creatures* the most ridiculous, and the soonest found out. It is good to be early in your Caution, to avoid any thing that cometh within distance of such despicable Patterns, and not like some *Ladies*, who defer their *Converſion*, till they have been ſo long in Poſſeſſion of being laughed at, that the World doth not know how to change their Style, even when they are reclaimed from that which gave the firſt Occaſion for it.

The Advantages of being reſerved are too many to be ſet down; I will only ſay, that it is a Guard to a *good Woman*, and a Diſguiſe to an *ill one*. It is of ſo much uſe to both, that thoſe ought to uſe it as an *Artifice*, who refuſe to practiſe it as a Virtue.

FRIENDSHIPS.

I Muſt in a particular manner recommend to you a ſtrict Care in the Choice of your *Friendſhips*. Perhaps the beſt are not without their *Objections*; but however, be ſure that yours may not ſtray from the Rules which the wiſer Part of the World hath ſet to them. The Leagues *Offenſive* and *Defenſive* ſeldom hold in *Politicks*, and much leſs in *Friendſhips*. The violent *Intimacies*, when once broken, of which they ſcarce ever fail, make ſuch a *Noiſe*; the Bag of Secrets untied, they fly about like Birds let looſe from a Cage, and become the *Entertainment* of the *Town*. Beſides, theſe great *Dearneſſes* by degrees grow *injurious* to the reſt of your *Acquaintance*, and throw them off from you. There is ſuch an *Offenſive* Diſtinction when the *dear Friend* cometh into the Room, that it is
flinging

flinging *Stones* at the *Company*, who are not apt to forgive it.

Do not lay out your *Friendship* too *lavishly* at first, since it will, like other things, be so much the sooner spent; neither let it be of too sudden a *Growth*; for as the Plants which shoot up too *fast* are not of that *Continuance*, as those which take more Time for it; so too swift a Progress in pouring out your *Kindness*, is a certain Sign that by the Course of Nature it will not be long-lived. You will be responsible to the World, if you pitch upon such *Friends* as at the time are under the Weight of any *criminal Objection*. In that Case you'll bring yourself under the Disadvantages of their *Character*, and must bear your Part of it. *Chusing* implieth *approving*; and if you fix upon a *Lady* for your *Friend* against whom the World shall have given Judgment, 'tis not so well-natur'd as to believe you are altogether *averse* to her way of *living*; since it doth not discourage

rage you from admitting her into your *Kindness*: And *Resemblance* of *Inclinations* being thought none of the least Inducements to *Friendship*, you will be looked upon at least as a Well-wisher, if not a Partner, with her in her Faults. If you can forgive them in another, it may be presumed you will not be less gentle to yourself; and therefore you must not take it ill, if you are reckoned a *Croupiere*, and condemned to pay an equal Share with such a Friend, of the *Reputation* she has lost.

If it happeneth that your *Friend* should fall from the State of *Innocence* after your Kindness was engaged to her, you may be slow in your Belief in the Beginning of the Discovery: But as soon as you are convinced by a *rational Evidence*, you must without breaking too roughly, make a fair and quick Retreat from such a *mistaken Acquaintance*: Else by moving too slowly from one that is so tainted, the Contagion may reach you

you so far, as to give you part of the *Scandal*, though not of the *Guilt*. This Matter is so nice, that as you must not be too hasty to join in the *Censure* upon your *Friend* when she is *accused*, so you are not, on the other Side, to *defend* her with too much Warmth; for if she should happen to deserve the Report of *common Fame*, besides the Vexation belonging to such a Mistake, you will draw an *ill Appearance* upon yourself, and it will be thought you pleaded for her not without some *Consideration* of yourself. The *Anger* which must be put on to vindicate the *Reputation* of an injur'd *Friend*, may incline the Company to suspect you would not be so *zealous*, if there was not a Possibility that the Case might be your own. For this Reason you are not to carry your *Dearness* so far, as absolutely to lose your Sight where your Friend is concerned. Because *Malice* is too quick-sighted, it doth not follow, that *Friendship* must be

blind:

blind: There is to be a *Mean* between these two *Extreams*, else your Excess of Good-Nature may betray you into a very *ridiculous Figure,* and by degrees you may be preferr'd to such Offices as you will not be proud of. Your *Ignorance* may lessen the *Guilt,* but will improve the *Jest* upon you, who shall be kindly solicitous to procure a Meeting, and innocently contribute to the *Ills* you would avoid: Whilst the *Contriving Lovers*, when they are alone, shall make you the Subject of their Mirth, and, perhaps, (with respect to the Goddess of *Love* be it spoken) it is not the worst part of their *Entertainment*, at least it is the most lasting, to laugh at the *believing Friend*, who was so easily deluded.

Let the good Sense of your *Friends* be a chief Ingredient in your *Choice* of them; else let your *Reputation* be never so clear, it may be clouded by their *Impertinence.* It is like our Houses being in the Power of a
drunken

drunken or a careless Neighbour; only so much worse, as that there will be no Insurance here to make you amends, as there is in the Case of Fire.

To conclude this Paragraph: If *Formality* is to be allowed in any Instance, it is to be put on to resist the Invasion of such forward Women as shall press themselves into your *Friendship*, where, if admitted, they will either be a Snare or an Incumbrance.

CENSURE.

Censure.

I Will next come to the Confideration, how you are to manage your *Censure*; in which both Care and Skill will be a good deal required. To diftinguifh is not only *natural* but *neceffary*; and the Effect of it is, That we cannot avoid giving Judgment in our Minds, either to *abfolve* or *condemn* as the Cafe requireth. The *Difficulty* is, to know when and where it is fit to *proclaim* the *Sentence*. An Averfion to what is *criminal*, a *Contempt* of what is *ridiculous*, are the infeparable *Companions* of Underftanding and Virtue; but the letting them go farther than our own *Thoughts*, hath fo much Danger in it, that though it is neither poffible nor fit to *fupprefs* them intirely, yet it is neceffary they fhould be kept under very great *Reftraints*. An *unlimited Liberty* of this kind, is little lefs than fending a *Herald* and proclaiming War to the World,

World, which is an *angry Beast* when so provoked. The Contest will be *unequal*, though you are never so much in the right: And if you begin against such an Adversary, it will tear you in Pieces, with this Justification, that it is done in its own Defence. You must therefore take heed of *laughing*, except in Company that is very sure. It is throwing Snow-balls against Bullets; and it is the *Disadvantage* of a Woman, that the Malice of the World will help the Brutality of those who will throw a *slovenly Untruth* upon her. You are for this Reason to suppress your *Impatience* for Fools; who, besides they are too strong a Party to be unnecessarily provoked, are of all others the most dangerous in this Case. A *Blockhead* in his *Rage* will return a *dull Jest* that will lie heavy, though there is not a *Grain* of *Wit* in it. Others will do it with more Art, and you must not think yourself secure because your *Reputation*

tation may, perhaps, be out of the reach of *Ill-will*; for if it findeth that Part *guarded*, it will seek one which is more exposed. It flieth, like a corrupt Humour in the Body, to the *weakest* Part. If you have a *tender Side*, the World will be sure to find it, and to put the worst *Colour* upon all you say or do, give an *Aggravation* to every thing that may lessen you, and a *spiteful Turn* to every thing that might recommend you. *Anger* layeth open those Defects which *Friendship* would not see, and *Civility* might be willing to forget; *Malice* needeth no such *Invitation* to encourage it, neither are any *Pains* more superfluous than those we take to be ill spoken of. If *Envy*, which never dieth, and seldom sleepeth, is content sometimes to be in a *Slumber*, it is very unskilful to make a noise to *awake* it.

Besides, your *Wit* will be misapplied if it is wholly directed to discern the *Faults* of *others*, when it is so neceſſary to be often uſed to *mend* and *prevent your own.* The ſending our *Thoughts* too much abroad hath the ſame Effect, as when a *Family* never ſtayeth at Home; *Neglect* and *Diſorder* naturally followeth; as it muſt do within ourſelves, if we do not frequently turn our Eyes inwards, to ſee what is amiſs with us, where it is a Sign we have an *unwelcome Proſpect,* when we do not care to *look* upon it, but rather ſeek our *Conſolations* in the *Faults* of thoſe we converſe with.

Avoid being the firſt in fixing a *hard Cenſure*; let it be confirmed by the general *Voice,* before you give into it; neither are you then to give Sentence like a *Magiſtrate,* or as if you had a *ſpecial Authority* to beſtow a *good* or *ill* Name at your Diſcretion. Do not dwell too long upon a *weak Side,* touch and go away; take Pleaſure to ſtay longer where you can commend: like *Bees* that fix only upon thoſe *Herbs* out of which they may

may extract the Juice of which their Honey is composed. A *Virtue* stuck with *Bristles* is too rough for this Age; it must be adorn'd with some *Flowers*, or else it will be unwillingly entertained; so that even where it may be fit to strike, do it like a *Lady*, gently; and assure yourself, that where you care to do it, you will wound others more, and hurt yourself less, by soft *Strokes*, than by being *harsh* or *violent*.

The Triumph of *Wit* is to make your *Good-Nature* subdue your *Censure*; to be quick in seeing *Faults*, and slow in exposing them. You are to consider, that the invisible Thing called a *Good Name*, is made up of the Breath of Numbers that speak well of you; so that if by a *disobliging Word* you silence the *Meanest*, the *Gale* will be less strong which is to bear up your *Esteem*; and though nothing is so vain as the eager Pursuit of *empty Applause*, yet to be well thought of, and to be kindly used by by the World, is like a *Glory* about a Woman's Head, 'tis a Perfume she carrieth about with her, and leaveth wherever she goeth; 'tis a Charm against *Ill-will*. *Malice* may empty her Quiver, but cannot wound; the Dirt will not stick, the Jests will not take: Without the Consent of the World a Scandal doth not go deep; it is only a slight Stroke upon the injured Party, and turneth with the greater Force upon those that gave it.

VANITY *and* AFFECTATION.

I Muſt with more than ordinary *Earneſtneſs* give you Caution againſt *Vanity*, it being the Fault to which your Sex ſeemeth to be moſt inclined; and ſince *Affectation* for the moſt part attendeth it, I do not know how to divide them. I will not call them *Twins*, becauſe more properly *Vanity* is the *Mother*, and *Affectation* is the *darling Daughter*; *Vanity* is the Sin, and *Affectation* is the *Puniſhment*; the firſt may be called the *Root* of *Self-love*, the other the *Fruit*. *Vanity* is never at its full growth till it ſpreadeth into *Affectation*, and then it is compleat.

Not to dwell any longer upon the Definition of them, I will paſs to the Means and Motives to avoid them. In order to it, you are to conſider that the World challengeth the Right of diſtributing Eſteem and Applauſe;

Applause; so that where any assume, by their single Authority, to be their own *Carvers*, it groweth angry, and never faileth to seek *Revenge*. And if we may measure a Fault by the Greatness of the *Penalty*, there are few of a higher Size than *Vanity*, as there is scarce a Punishment which can be heavier than that of being laughed at.

Vanity maketh a Woman tainted with it, so top-full of herself, that she spilleth it upon the *Company*. And because her own Thoughts are intirely employ'd in *Self-Contemplation*, she endeavoureth by a cruel Mistake, to confine her *Acquaintance* to the same narrow Circle of that which only concerneth her Ladyship, forgetting that she is not of half that *Importance* to the World that she is to herself; so mistaken she is in her Value, by being her own Appraiser. She will fetch such a Compass in *Discourse*, to bring in her *beloved Self*, and rather than fail, her fine Petticoat, that there can hardly be a better Scene than such a Trial of ridiculous Ingenuity. It is a Pleasure to see her angle for *Commendations*, and rise so dissatisfied with the Ill-bred *Company* if they will not *bite*. To observe her throwing her *Eyes* about to fetch in Prisoners, and go about cruizing like a Privateer, and so out of *Countenance*, if she return without *Booty*, is no ill Piece of Comedy. She is so eager to draw Respect, that she always misseth it, yet thinketh it so much her due, that when she faileth, she groweth *waspish*, not considering, that it is impossible to commit a Rape upon the Will; that it must be fairly gained, and will not be taken by *Storm*; and that in this Case, the Tax ever riseth highest by a *Benevolence*. If the World, instead of admiring her *imaginary Excellencies*, taketh the Liberty to laugh at them, she *appealeth* from it to herself, for whom she giveth *Sentence*, and proclaimeth

claimeth it in all Companies. On the other Side, if encouraged by a *civil Word*, she is so obliging, that she will give Thanks for being laughed at in good Language. She taketh a *Compliment* for a *Demonstration*, and setteth it up as an *Evidence*, even against her Looking-glass. But the good *Lady* being all this while in a most profound *Ignorance* of herself, forgetteth that Men would not let her talk upon them, and throw so many senseless Words at their Head, if they did not intend to put her Person to Fine and Ransom for her *Impertinence*. Good Words of any other *Lady*, are so many Stones thrown at her, she can by no means bear them; they make her so uneasy, that she cannot keep her *Seat*, but up she riseth and goeth Home half burst with *Anger* and *Strait-Lacing*. If by great chance she saith any thing that hath Sense in it, she expecteth such an excessive Rate of *Commendations*, that, to her thinking, the Company ever
                                                                                                        riseth

riseth in her *Debt.* She looketh upon *Rules* as Things made for the common People, and not for Persons of her *Rank*; and this Opinion sometimes tempteth her to extend her Prerogative to the dispensing with the Commandments. If by great Fortune she happeneth, in spite of her *Vanity*, to be honest, she is so troublesome with it, that as far as in her lieth, she maketh a scurvy Thing of it. Her bragging of her *Virtue*, looketh as if it cost her so much Pains to get the better of herself, that the *Inferences* are very ridiculous. Her good Humour is generally applied to the laughing at *good Sense.* It would do one good to see how heartily she despiseth any thing that is fit for her to do. The greatest Part of her *Fancy* is laid out in chusing her *Gown*, as her *Discretion* is chiefly employed in *not paying* for it. She is faithful to the *Fashion*, to which not only her *Opinion*, but her *Senses* are wholly resigned: So obsequious she is to it, it, that we should be ready to be reconciled even to *Virtue* with all its Faults, if she had her Dancing-Master's Word that it was practised at Court.

To a Woman so composed, when *Affectation* cometh in to improve her *Character*, it is then raised to the highest *Perfection*. She first setteth up for a *fine Thing*, and for that Reason will distinguish herself right or wrong, in every thing she doth. She would have it thought that she is made of so much the *finer Clay*, and so much more *sifted* than ordinary, that she hath no *common Earth* about her. To this end she must neither *move* nor *speak* like other Women, because it would be *vulgar*; and therefore must have a Language of her *own*, since *ordinary English* is too coarse for her. The *Looking-Glass* in the Morning dictateth to her all the *Motions* of the Day, which by how much the more *studied*, are so much the more *mistaken*. She cometh
into

into a Room as if her Limbs were set on with ill-made Screws, which maketh the Company fear the pretty Thing should leave some of its *Artificial Person* upon the Floor. She doth not like herself as *God Almighty* made her, but will have some of *her own* Workmanship; which is so far from making her a better Thing than a *Woman*, that it turneth her into a worse Creature than a *Monkey*. She falleth out with *Nature*, against which she maketh War without admitting a *Truce*, those Moments excepted in which her *Gallant* may reconcile her to it. When she hath a mind to be *soft* and *languishing*, there is something so unnatural in that *affected Easiness*, that her Frowns could not be by many Degrees so forbidding. When she would appear unreasonably *Humble*, one may see she is so excessively *Proud*, that there is no enduring it. There is such an *impertinent Smile*, such a *satisfied Simper*, when she faintly disowneth some fulsome

fulsome Commendation a Man happeneth to bestow upon her against his Conscience, that her *Thanks* for it are more visible under such a thin *Disguise*, than they could be if she should *print* them. If a *handsomer Woman* taketh any liberty of *Dressing* out of the ordinary Rules, the mistaken Lady followeth, without distinguishing the unequal *Pattern*, and maketh herself *uglier* by an Example misplaced; either forgetting the Privilege of *good Looks* in *another*, or presuming, without sufficient Reason, upon her *own*. Her *Discourse* is a *senseless Chime* of *empty Words*, a Heap of *Compliments* so equally applied to differing *Persons*, that they are neither valued nor believed. Her *Eyes* keep pace with her *Tongue*, and are therefore always in Motion. One may discern that they generally incline to the *compassionate* Side, and that, notwithstanding her Pretence to *Virtue*, she is gentle to distressed *Lovers* and *Ladies* that are *merciful*.

She

She will repeat the tender Part of a *Play* so feelingly, that the Company may guess without Injustice, she was not altogether a *disinterested Spectator*. She thinketh that *Paint* and *Sin* are conceal'd by railing at them. Upon the latter she is less hard, and being divided between the two opposite Prides of her *Beauty* and her *Virtue*, she is often tempted to give broad Hints that somebody is dying for her; and of the two, she is less unwilling to let the World think she may be sometimes *profan'd*, than that she is never *worshipped*.

Very great *Beauty* may perhaps so dazzle for a time, that Men may not so clearly see the *Deformity* of these *Affectations*; but when the *Brightness* goeth off, and that the *Lover*'s *Eyes* are by that Means set at liberty to see Things as they are, he will naturally return to his Senses, and recover the Mistake into which the Lady's *good Looks* had at first engaged him. And being once undeceived, ceaseth to worship that as a *Goddess* which he seeth only an *Artificial Shrine* moved by *Wheels* and *Springs*, to delude him. Such Women please only like the *first opening* of a *Scene*, that hath nothing to recommend it but the being *new*. They may be compared to Flies, that have pretty shining *Wings* for two or three hot Months, but the first cold Weather maketh an end of them; so the *latter Season* of these *fluttering Creatures* is dismal: From their nearest Friends they receive a very faint Respect; from the rest of the World, the utmost degree of Contempt.

Let this *Picture* supply the Place of any other *Rules* which might be given to prevent your *Resemblance* to it. The *Deformity* of it, well considered, is *Instruction* enough; from the same Reason, that the Sight of a *Drunkard* is a better *Sermon* against that *Vice*, than the best that was ever preached upon that *Subject*.

PRIDE.

PRIDE.

AFTER having said this against *Vanity*, I do not intend to apply the same *Censure* to *Pride*, well placed and rightly defined. It is an *ambiguous Word*; one kind of it is as much a *Virtue* as the other is a *Vice*: But we are naturally so apt to choose the *worst*, that it is become dangerous to commend the *best* Side of it.

A Woman is not to be proud of her fine Gown; nor when she hath less Wit than her Neighbours, to comfort herself that she hath more Lace. Some Ladies put so much Weight upon *Ornaments*, that if one could see into their Hearts, it would be found, that even the Thoughts of *Death* is made less heavy to them by the Contemplation of their being laid out in State, and *honourably attended* to the *Grave*. One may come a good deal short of such an *Extream*,

tream, and yet still be sufficiently *impertinent*, by setting a wrong Value upon things, which ought to be used with more Indifference. A Lady must not appear solicitous to ingross *Respect* to herself, but be content with a reasonable *Distribution*, and allow it to others, that she may have it returned to her. She is not to be troublesomely *Nice*, nor distinguish herself by being too *Delicate*, as if ordinary things were *too coarse* for her; this is an *unmannerly* and an *offensive Pride*, and where it is practised, deserveth to be mortified, of which it seldom faileth. She is not to lean too much upon her Quality, much less to despise those who are below it. Some make *Quality* an *Idol*, and then their *Reason* must fall down and worship it. They would have the World think, that no Amends can ever be made for the want of a *great Title*, or an antient *Coat of Arms:* They imagine, that with these *Advantages* they stand

upon

PRIDE.

upon the higher *Ground*, which maketh them look down upon *Merit* and *Virtue* as Things inferior to them. This Mistake is not only *senseless*, but *criminal* too, in putting a greater Price upon that which is a Piece of *good Luck*, than upon Things which are valuable in themselves. *Laughing* is not enough for such a *Folly*; it must be severely *whipped*, as it justly deserves. It will be confessed, there are frequent *Temptations* given by *pert Upstarts* to be Angry, and by that to have our Judgments corrupted in these Cases: But they are to be resisted; and the utmost that is to be allowed, is when those of a *new Edition* will forget themselves, so as either to brag of their *weak Side*, or to endeavour to hide their *Meanness* by their *Insolence*, to cure them by a little seasonable *Raillery*, a little *Sharpness* well placed, without dwelling too long upon it.

These and many other Kinds of *Pride* are to be avoided.

That which is to be recommended to you, is an Emulation to raise yourself to a Character, by which you may be distinguished; an Eagerness for Precedence in *Virtue*, and all such other Things as may gain you a greater Share of the good Opinion of the World. *Esteem* to *Virtue* is like a *cherishing Air* to *Plants* and *Flowers*, which maketh them blow and prosper: and for that Reason it may be allowed to be in some Degree the Cause as well as the *Reward* of it. That *Pride* which leadeth to a *good End*, cannot be a *Vice*, since it is the beginning of a *Virtue*; and to be pleased with just *Applause*, is so far from a *Fault*, that it would be an *ill Symptom* in a Woman, who should not place the greatest part of her *Satisfaction* on it. *Humility* is no doubt a great *Virtue*; but it ceaseth to be so, when it is afraid to scorn an *ill Thing*. Against *Vice* and *Folly* it is becoming your *Sex* to be *haughty*; but you must not carry the *Contempt* of
Things

Things to *Arrogance* towards Perſons, and it muſt be done with fitting *Diſtinctions*, elſe it may be *inconvenient* by being *unſeaſonable*. A *Pride* that raiſeth a little *Anger* to be outdone in any thing that is *good*, will have ſo good an Effect, that it is very hard to allow it to be a *Fault*.

It is no eaſy matter to carry even between theſe different Kinds deſcrib'd; but remember that it is ſafer for a *Woman* to be thought too *proud*, than too *familiar*.

DIVERSIONS.

THE laſt Thing I ſhall recommend to you, is a wiſe and a ſafe Method of uſing *Diverſions*. To be too eager in the Purſuit of Pleaſure whilſt you are *young*, is dangerous; to catch at it in riper *Years*, is graſping a Shadow; it will not be held. Beſides, that by being leſs natural it groweth to be indecent. *Diverſions* are the moſt properly applied, to eaſe and relieve thoſe who are *Oppreſſed*, by being too much employed. Thoſe that are *Idle* have no need of them, and yet they, above all others, give themſelves up to them. To unbend our *Thoughts*, when they are too much ſtretched by our *Cares*, is not more natural than it is neceſſary, but to turn our whole Lives into a *Holyday*, is not only *ridiculous*, but *deſtroyeth* Pleaſure inſtead of *promoting* it. The *Mind*

Mind like the *Body* is tired by being always in one Posture, too serious breaketh, and too diverting loofeneth it: It is *Variety* that giveth the Relish; so that *Diversions* too frequently repeated, grow first to be indifferent, and at last tedious: Whilst they are well-chosen and well-timed, they are never to be blamed; but when they are used to an Excess, though very *innocent* at first, they often grow to be *criminal*, and never fail to be *impertinent*.

Some Ladies are bespoken for Merry Meetings, as *Bessus* was for Duels. They are engaged in a Circle of *Idleness*, where they turn round for the whole Year, without the *Interruption* of a serious Hour. They know all the Players Names, and are *intimately* acquainted with all the Booths in *Bartholomew-Fair*. No Soldier is more obedient to the sound of his Captain's *Trumpet*, than they are to that which summoneth them to a *Puppet-Play* or a *Monster*.

The

The Spring that bringeth out *Flies* and *Fools*, maketh them Inhabitants in *Hyde-Park*; in the Winter they are an Incumbrance to the *Play-house*, and the Ballast of the *Drawing-room*. The Streets all this while are so weary of these daily Faces, that *Mens Eyes* are overlaid with them. The Sight is glutted with fine things, as the *Stomach* with sweet ones; and when a fair *Lady* will give too much of herself to the World, she groweth luscious, and oppresseth instead of pleasing. These *jolly Ladies* do so continually seek *Diversion*, that in a little Time they grow into a *Jest*, yet are unwilling to remember, that if they were seldomer seen, they would not be so often *laughed at*. Besides, they make themselves *cheap*, than which there cannot be an *unkinder* Word bestowed upon your *Sex*.

To Play sometimes, to entertain *Company*, or to divert yourself, is not to be disallowed; but to do it
so

so often as to be called a *Gamester*, is to be avoided, next to the things that are most *criminal*. It hath Consequences of *several Kinds* not to be endured; it will engage you into a Habit of *Idleness* and *ill Hours*, draw you into a mix'd Company, make you neglect your *Civilities* Abroad, and your *Business* at Home, and impose into your *Acquaintance* such as will do you no Credit.

To deep *Play* there will be yet greater *Objections*: It will give *Occasion* to the World to ask *spiteful Questions*: How you dare venture to *lose*, and what Means you have to pay such great *Sums*? If you pay *exactly*, it will be enquired from whence the *Money* cometh? If you owe, and especially to a Man, you must be so very *civil* to him for his Forbearance, that it layeth a Ground of having it farther improved, if the *Gentleman* is so disposed; who will be thought no unfair *Creditor*, if where the *Estate* faileth he seizeth
upon

upon the Person. Besides, if a *Lady* could see her own Face upon an *ill Game*, at a deep Stake, she would certainly forswear any thing that could put her Looks under such a *Disadvantage*.

To *Dance* sometimes will not be imputed to you as a Fault; but remember, that the End of your learning it was, that you might the better know how to *move gracefully*. It is only an *Advantage* so far; when it goeth beyond it, one may call it *excelling* in a Mistake, which is no very great Commendation. It is better for a *Woman* never to *dance*, because she hath no Skill in it, than to do it too often, because she doth it well. The easiest as well as the safest *Method* of doing it, is in *private Companies*, amongst *particular Friends*, and then carelesly like a *Diversion*, rather than with *Solemnity*, as if it was a Business, or had any thing in it to deserve a *Month's Preparation*, by serious Conference with a *Dancing-Master*.

Much

DIVERSIONS. 115

Much more might be said to all these Heads, and many more might be added to them: But I must restrain my Thoughts, which are full of my *Dear Child*, and would overflow into a Volume which would not be fit for a *New-Year's Gift*: I will conclude with my warmest Wishes for all that is good to you; that you may live so as to be an Ornament to your Family, and a Pattern to your Sex. That you may be blessed with a Husband that may value, and Children that may inherit your *Virtue*; that you may shine in the World by a true Light, and silence Envy by deserving to be esteemed; that Wit and Virtue may both conspire to make you a great Figure: When they are separated, the first is so empty, and the other so faint, that they scarce have right to be commended. May they therefore meet and never part; let them be your Guardian Angels, and be sure never to stray out of the Distance

stance of their joint Protection. May you so raise your Character, that you may help to make the next Age a better thing, and leave Posterity in your Debt for the Advantage it shall receive by your Example.

Let me conjure you, *my Dearest*, to comply with this kind Ambition of a Father, whose Thoughts are so engaged in your behalf, that he reckoneth your Happiness to be the greatest Part of his own.

F I N I S.

BOOKS Printed for J. DODSLEY.

THE
PRECEPTOR:

Containing

A General Courſe of EDUCATION, Wherein the Firſt Principles of Polite Learning are laid down in a Way moſt ſuitable for trying the Genius, and advancing the Inſtruction of YOUTH.

In TWELVE PARTS, viz.

1. On Reading, Speaking, and Writing Letters.
2. On Geometry.
3. On Geography and Aſtronomy.
4. On Chronology and Hiſtory.
5. On Rhetoric and Poetry.
6. On Drawing.
7. On Logic.
8. On Natural Hiſtory.
9. On Ethics, or Morality.
10. On Trade and Commerce.
11. On Laws and Government.
12. On Human Life and Manners.

Illuſtrated with MAPS and uſeful CUTS.

A new Tranſlation of Don Quixote, by the late Mr. Jarvis, in 2 vol. 4to. Adorned with 69 Copper-Plates, deſign'd by Vanderbank, and engrav'd by Vandergucht; with a curious Preface and Notes by the Tranſlator, an Account of the Cuts by Dr. Oldfield, and the Life of Cervantes, tranſlated from the Spaniſh of Don Gregorio de Meyans Siſcar,

BOOKS Printed for J. Dodsley.

Sifcar, Library Keeper to the King of Spain. Written at the Requeſt of the Earl of Granville. Price 2*l.* 10*s.*

Les Avantures de Telemaque, Fils d'Ulyſſe, in two neat Pocket Volumes, printed on a ſuperfine Writing Paper, with an Elziver Letter, and a Compleat Set of new Cuts, 26 in Number, done from the Deſigns of that fine Edition printed in Holland, and engraved by the beſt Maſters. Being a very handſome Preſent for young Gentlemen or Ladies at Boarding Schools. Price 14*s.*

Circe, tranſlated from the Italian of John Baptiſt Gelli, of the Academy of Florence. Price 4*s.*

The Decameron, or one Hundred ingenious and diverting Novels. Written originally in Italian by John Boccace, newly tranſlated into Engliſh by a Gentleman. In 1 vol. 8vo. 6*s.*

N. B. Theſe beautiful Stories are divided into Ten Days Entertainment, Ten Novels for each Day. 1. On various Subjects. 2. and 3. Great Troubles and perplex'd Adventures crown'd with Succeſs. 4. Such Amours and Love Adventures as have had an unfortunate Concluſion. 5. Amours and Love Adventures that have ended happily. 6. Subjects of Wit and Humour. 7. and 8. Stratagems that Women have contriv'd to deceive their Huſbands. 9. Miſcellaneous Novels. 10. Gallant or generous Actions done for the Sake of a Miſtreſs, a Friend, &c.

In

BOOKS Printed for J. DODSLEY.

In Seven Parts compleat, 1s. The Seventh Edition, of the Œconomy of Human Life, tranflated from an Indian Manufcript. Written by an ancient Bramin. 1. Duties that relate to Man confidered as an Individual, viz. Confideration, Modefty, Application, Emulation, Prudence, Contentment, Temperance. 2. Of the Paffions. Hope and Fear, Joy and Grief, Anger, Pity, Defire and Love. 3. Woman. 4. Confanguinity, or Natural Relations, viz. Hufband, Father, Son, Brother. 5. Providence, or the Accidental Differences of Men, viz. Wife and Ignorant, Rich and Poor, Mafters and Servants, Magiftrates and Subjects. 6. Social Duties, viz. Benevolence, Juftice, Charity, Gratitude, Sincerity. 7. Religion. Alfo, for the Ufe of Schools, 2s. bound, the fame Book in French and Englifh; the French Tranflation made by Command of his late Serene Highnefs the Prince of Orange, for the Ufe of his Daughter the Princefs Caroline. Likewife a Tranflation of the fame into Latin, and another into Italian.

Letters concerning Tafte, 8vo. 2s.

Poems, by Mr. Thomas Blacklock, with an Account of the Author, by Mr. Spence, 8vo. 5s.

A Collection of the beft and moft entertaining Voyages and Travels, 7 vol. 12mo. 1l. 1s.

The Praifes of Ifis, a Poem, 4to. 1s.

The

BOOKS Printed for J. Dodsley.

The World, by Adam Fitz-Adam, in 6 vol. 12mo. 1*l.* 1*s.*

Chit Chat, or natural Characters and the Manners of real Life, represented in a feries of entertaining Adventures, 2 vol. 12mo. 5*s.*

A Dictionary of the English Language, wherein the Signification of Words are illustrated by Examples from the best English Writers; 2 vol. folio, 4*l.* 10*s.* and an Abridgment of the same Work in which the Examples are excluded, in 2 vol. 8vo. 10*s.*

British Education, being an Attempt to shew that a Revival of the Art of Speaking, and the Study of our own Language, might contribute, in a great Measure, to the Cure of those Evils which are the necessary Consequences of the present defective System of Education in general, and of the Neglect of this Study in particular, by Thomas Sheridan, M. A. 8vo. 6*s.*

A new History of the East-Indies, ancient and modern, giving an Account of the Religion, Government, Manners and Customs, natural History, Revolutions, &c. of these Countries, and also an Account of the Rife, Progress, and present State of the Commerce of the Europeans to the Indies, 2 vol. 8vo. 10*s.*

A Philosophical Enquiry into the Origin of our Ideas of the Sublime and Beautiful, 8vo. 5*s.*

A free Enquiry into the Nature and Origin of Evil, in 6 Letters, 2*s.*

The Adventurer, 4 vol. 12mo. 12*s.*

www.ingramcontent.com/pod-product-compliance
Lightning Source LLC
Chambersburg PA
CBHW022142160426
43197CB00009B/1396